Science and Technology
Buildings and Structures

Andrew Solway

www.raintreepublishers.co.uk

Visit our website to find out more information about Raintree books.

To order:

☎ Phone 0845 6044371
🖷 Fax +44 (0) 1865 312263
🖳 Email myorders@raintreepublishers.co.uk

Customers from outside the UK please telephone +44 1865 312262

Raintree is an imprint of Capstone Global Library Limited, a company incorporated in England and Wales having its registered office at 7 Pilgrim Street, London, EC4V 6LB – Registered company number: 6695582

Text © Capstone Global Library Limited 2012
First published in hardback in 2012
The moral rights of the proprietor have been asserted.

Edited by Andrew Farrow, Adam Miller, and Diyan Leake
Designed by Victoria Allen
Original illustrations © Capstone Global Library Ltd 2011
Illustrated by Oxford Designers and Illustrators
Picture research by Elizabeth Alexander
Originated by Capstone Global Library Ltd
Printed and bound in China by CTPS

ISBN 978 1 406 22838 0 (hardback)
15 14 13 12 11
10 9 8 7 6 5 4 3 2 1

British Library Cataloguing in Publication Data
Solway, Andrew.
  Science and technology: buildings and structures.
-- (Sci-hi)
  720.1'05-dc22
A full catalogue record for this book is available from the British Library.

Acknowledgements

The author and publishers are grateful to the following for permission to reproduce copyright material: Alamy pp. **18** (© Stock Connection Blue/Arthur Ruffino), **20** (© Mathias Beinling), **29** (© Peter Tsai Photography), **30** (© Christine Osborne Pictures), **32** (© m-images); © Arup www.arup.com p. **40**; Bharani Padmanabhan MD PhD p. **38**; © Bob Cortright, Bridge Ink p. **7**; Corbis pp. **17** (© Brad Schloss/Icon SMI), **24** (© Charlotte Wood/Arcaid), **27** (© Proehl Studios), **35** (© Alejandro Bolivar/epa); Getty Images pp. **4** (Kimberly White/Bloomberg), **5** (Mori Building Co.), **9** (Kevin Phillips), **23** (Joel Saget/AFP); NASA (Goddard Space Flight Center Scientific Visualization Studio, United States Geological Survey) p. **33** top, bottom; Photolibrary pp. **6** (Photo Channel), **12** (Jim Wark), **21** (View Pictures/Chris Gascoigne), **22** (Martin Siepmann), **26** (Martin Bond), **34** (Jane Sweeney), **37** (Martin Page), **39** (Thomas Frey); Reuters p. **25** (Ho New); Shutterstock **contents page** top (© Patrick Wang), **contents page** bottom (© MaxFX), pp. **10** (© Mumbojumbo), **13** (© Patrick Wang), **14** (© Peter Zaharov), **15** (© MaxFX), **16** (© Rob Wilson), **19** (© leungchopan), **31** (© Bertl123), **all background and design features**.

Main cover photograph of the China National Olympic Stadium reproduced with permission of shutterstock (© Eastimages); inset cover photograph of grass on a football pitch reproduced with permission of shutterstock (© Lario Tus).

The publisher would like to thank literary consultant Nancy Harris and content consultant Suzy Gazlay for their assistance in the preparation of this book.

Every effort has been made to contact copyright holders of material reproduced in this book. Any omissions will be rectified in subsequent printings if notice is given to the publisher.

Disclaimer

All the Internet addresses (URLs) given in this book were valid at the time of going to press. However, due to the dynamic nature of the Internet, some addresses may have changed, or sites may have changed or ceased to exist since publication. While the author and publisher regret any inconvenience this may cause readers, no responsibility for any such changes can be accepted by either the author or the publisher.

Contents

Some words are shown in bold, **like this**. These words are explained in the glossary. You will find important information and definitions underlined, <u>like this</u>.

What makes arches so strong? Read page 13 to find out!

Where is this building with many domes? Turn to page 15 to find out!

INTRODUCTION

A crane operator sits in a small glass cabin 100 metres above the city. The people below look smaller than ants. The operator moves control levers and the crane lifts a large concrete panel. As the panel rises, the wind catches it and it begins to swing. The operator quickly adjusts the controls. The panel stops swinging. The operator lowers it carefully on to the top of the growing skyscraper.

When you are building a skyscraper, crane operators are important people. They lift all the materials into place. Architects are important, too. They design the building and decide how it should look. But the people who really matter are the **engineers**. They make sure that the building stays up.

Tower cranes work on the Oakland Bay Bridge in San Francisco, USA.

Engineers

All large construction projects need engineers. They build towers, bridges, tunnels, and dams. Engineers make sure that a structure is strong enough to stand up to storms, high winds, floods, and even earthquakes.

Some structures built by engineers are so big they can be seen from the Moon. Others were built so well that they have survived 3,000 years.

The World Financial Centre in Shanghai is one of the tallest buildings in the world. It has a "window" through the top of the building.

AMAZING CRANES

- The strongest crane in the world is called "Taisun". It is the main crane in the Yantai Raffles shipyard in China. It can lift over 20,000 tonnes.

- The highest cranes in the world were used to build the Burj Khalifa (Khalifa Tower) in Dubai (see page 22). Builders were working over 800 metres (2,625 feet) above ground.

- The biggest mobile crane in the world is the Mammoet "Momo". It can lift up to 1,600 tonnes.

- The world's tallest tower crane is the Kroll K-10 000. It can lift objects to a height of 120 metres (394 feet).

STRUNG ON A WIRE

Suppose you have to build a bridge across a strait (narrow stretch of sea). The strait is about 4 kilometres (2.5 miles) wide and 100 metres (328 feet) deep, with fast-flowing currents. It is a very busy sea route, with over 1,000 ships passing through every day. The bridge has to stand up to hurricane-force winds and severe earthquakes. And there must be as few bridge supports as possible, so that ships can pass under it easily.

The Akashi Kaikyo Bridge

This was the challenge for the Japanese engineers building the Akashi Kaikyo Bridge. It took 2 million workers over 10 years to build. Part-way through construction, an earthquake tested the bridge design to its limits. But in 1998, the bridge was completed. It has the longest single span (distance from one end to the other) of any bridge in the world.

The Akashi Kaikyo Bridge is built to withstand high winds and strong earthquakes.

Spanning big gaps

The Akashi Kaikyo Bridge is a **suspension bridge**. Suspension bridges can span large gaps with no ground support. The simplest of all suspension bridges would be a cable (rope) strung between two anchor points. Some small suspension bridges are like this, with a few ropes strung across a river or **gorge** (deep valley). The anchor points have to be very strong, because they carry all the weight of the bridge.

A road or rail suspension bridge is more complicated. It has two main cables, anchored on either side of the gap. Instead of hanging across the gap, the cables go over two support towers, which lift them high into the air. These towers take part of the bridge's weight. The road or railway is hung from the main cables by many smaller support cables called **hangers**.

WHO DID THAT? THE FIRST SUSPENSION BRIDGE

The **Incas** of Peru made the earliest suspension bridges. They were built from ropes made of grass. The bridges had to be re-made once a year because the ropes stretched with time. Villagers had the job of rebuilding their local bridges.

The Keshwa Chaca is a grass-rope suspension bridge across the Apurimac River in Peru. Local villagers still rebuild the Keshwa Chaca every year.

Building a suspension bridge

The first parts of a suspension bridge to be built are the **foundations (base) of the towers**. These often have to be built under water. To make underwater foundations, engineers sink wide metal or concrete tubes into the river or seabed. They are filled with concrete once in place.

Next come the support towers, and the anchor points for the cables. The support towers are usually built from steel or concrete sections, one on top of the other. The anchor points are huge blocks of concrete fixed into solid rock.

AKASHI KAIKYO BRIDGE FACTS

Length: **3,911 metres (12,831 feet)**

Central span: **1,989 metres (6,525 feet)**

Height of towers: **283 metres (928 feet) – almost as high as the Eiffel Tower in France**

Cables: **there is enough steel cable to stretch 7½ times round the world**

Spinning the cables

Once the anchor points and towers are in place, the cables can be strung across the gap. The main cables for the Akashi Kaikyo Bridge are over 1 metre (3 feet 4 inches) thick and weigh 50,000 tonnes. Stringing something this heavy across the huge gap would be impossible. So the cable is put together from 580 separate strands. Each strand is carried across the gap by a special wheel hanging from a small guide cable. The wheel travels back and forth across the bridge, pulling strands of the main cable with it.

cable made up
of many strands

The main cables
on the Tsing Ma
suspension bridge
in Hong Kong are
1.1 metres (3 feet
7 inches) thick.

Hanging the deck

Once the two main cables are in place, the smaller
hanger cables can be hung from them. The **deck** of the
bridge (the road or railway track) is attached to the hangers. The Akashi
Kaikyo Bridge has special stiffening pieces fastened below the main
deck. The stiffening sections stop the roadway from shaking up and
down or twisting in high winds.

GIRDERS, TRUSSES, AND CANTILEVERS

In 2004, the tallest bridge in the world opened to the public. The Millau Viaduct crosses the River Tarn Gorge in southern France. The highest of the seven towers holding it up is 343 metres (1,125 feet) tall.

The Millau Viaduct looks quite like a suspension bridge. But in fact it is a cable-stayed bridge. <u>In a cable-stayed bridge, the deck is held up by a large number of cables attached directly to the towers</u>. All the weight is carried by these support towers.

BRIGHT IDEAS: SLIDING THE ROAD OUT

The roadway for the Millau Viaduct was built in two sections, one on either side of the valley. The two sections were then slowly slid out from the valley sides on to the support towers.

The Millau Viaduct has the longest cable-stayed deck in the world. It is nearly 2.5 kilometres (1½ miles) long.

Types of bridge

These diagrams show how the different types of bridge work.

Suspension bridge. This is explained on pages 7 to 9.

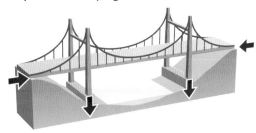

The Millau Viaduct (page 10) is an example of a *cable-stayed bridge*.

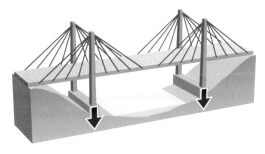

Each part of a *cantilever bridge* has a central support pillar, with bridge sections (cantilevers) balancing each other on either side. The Forth Rail Bridge in Scotland is a cantilever bridge.

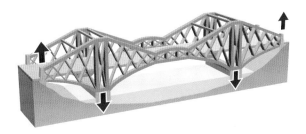

BRIGHT IDEAS: MOVING BRIDGES

Some bridges have to be able to move, usually to allow ships to pass:

- **Swing bridges** swing round on a single point. Often the bridge has two sections, balanced on either side of the central pivot.

- **Tilt bridges** have one or both ends of the bridge lifting up. Tower Bridge in London is a famous example.

Truss bridges have a framework of criss-crossing beams. The framework is strong but light.

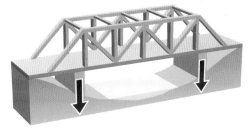

An *arch bridge* is supported by a large arch. See pages 12 to 13 for more on arches.

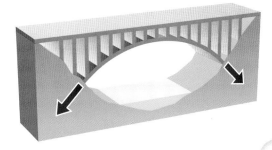

ARCHES

The Gateway Arch in St Louis is a gleaming metal curve that soars over 190 metres (630 feet) above the city. It is one of the most famous landmarks in the United States. The Gateway Arch makes a beautiful shape against the sky. But it is not arched just to look pretty. An arch is naturally a very strong shape – if it is made properly.

Different kinds of arch

A heavy weight in the middle of a beam makes it sag and break. <u>But a heavy weight on top of an arch compresses (squashes) the arch, which actually makes it stronger</u>.

Different arch shapes have different uses. A shallow arch is good for spanning a wide gap. However it does not take heavy weight so well. It can bulge outwards if it is not supported at the sides. Taller arches are better at transferring weight downwards without bulging.

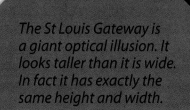

The St Louis Gateway is a giant optical illusion. It looks taller than it is wide. In fact it has exactly the same height and width.

Keystones and computers

In the past, arches were made from bricks or blocks of stone. <u>A stone or brick arch cannot support any weight until the top stone or brick (the keystone) is in place</u>. So these arches had to be built on a wooden frame, which was removed when the arch was completed.

Modern arches are often built from concrete or steel. They are made in large sections rather than small blocks. Engineers can make a "model" of an arch design on a computer, before they actually build it. They can use this to find where the structure needs to be strongest.

It is easy to see the wedge-shaped stones that make up each arch In the Mezquita (mosque) in Cordoba, Spain .

WHO DID THAT? CONCRETE ARCHES

Reinforced concrete <u>is concrete strengthened with steel bars</u>. It is one of the most important modern building materials. In the 1930s, Swiss engineer Robert Maillart began to use reinforced concrete in a whole new way. He built elegant arched bridges out of reinforced concrete. The style of Maillart's bridges has been copied around the world.

FROM ARCHES TO DOMES

In 1420, work began on a dome for the cathedral in Florence, Italy. It was to be 44 metres (115 feet) across. This was bigger than any dome that had ever been built before. The base of the dome was 52 metres (171 feet) above ground. This was too high to build a wooden frame to support the dome while it was being built. The job looked impossible.

The massive bulk of Il Duomo ("The Dome") dominates the cathedral in Florence.

Il Duomo

The man in charge of building the dome was Filippo Brunelleschi (1377–1446). Before he even started building, he had to invent two cranes to lift and place stone blocks for the dome. The cranes were the first of his many inventions. To stop the upper parts of the dome from falling inwards, Brunelleschi worked out a special zig-zag pattern for the bricks. Each brick was linked to the ones above and below it. This design helped hold the whole structure together.

The dome was finished in 1436. It is still the biggest brick dome ever built. Today Florence cathedral is usually called "Il Duomo" – the dome.

Domes and vaults

Domes and vaults are three-dimensional versions of arches. <u>A vault is like a set of arches in a straight line. A dome is like a set of arches that cross over in the middle</u>. As with an arch, the curved shape of a dome or vault allows it to span wide gaps. Vaulting is used for the roofs of many churches and great cathedrals.

Only a few European churches have domes like Il Duomo. However, many Islamic mosques are built around a large central dome.

The Blue Mosque in Istanbul, Turkey has many domes.

The glass-domed Feria Valencia centre in Spain has 7,700 square metres (82,900 square feet) of space for conferences and other events.

Modern domes

In the 20th century, new materials and designs made it possible to build domes far larger than in the past. The first new design was called a **geodesic dome**. This is a dome shape made from a series of connected triangles. Even very large geodesic domes are fairly lightweight structures. The Epcot Center in Florida, USA and the Eden Project in Cornwall are both geodesic domes.

Other kinds of domes have a lightweight shell. The shell can be made of concrete or steel. However, some domes use lighter materials such as **fibreglass**, plastic, or Kevlar (a super-strong material used in bullet-proof vests).

Domed sports arenas

The biggest modern domes are over sports arenas. One of the first was the Astrodome baseball park in Texas, USA. However, this domed roof was not a success. The clear plastic made the ballpark too bright in sunlight. The problem was solved by painting over parts of the roof. But then the grass did not grow properly. The ballpark had to be covered with artificial grass – "astroturf". Modern stadiums have a roof that can be opened and closed. This helps the grass grow better.

The domed roof of the Cowboys Stadium is the largest in the world.

BIGGEST DOME

The Cowboys Stadium in Texas is the home of the Dallas Cowboys American football team. The roof spans 275 metres (902 feet). It covers an area of 900,000 square metres (3 million square feet).

TOUGH ON GRASS

Keeping the grass healthy in a stadium is a tough task. Because of the stadium walls, the grass is in shade for large parts of the day. The grass can also get very hot in sunny conditions, and it is damaged by the sports that take place there. Special types of grass have been developed for growing in stadiums, but they need a lot of looking after.

Building high

The World Fair in New York, USA in 1854 was a showcase for new ideas for industry. The biggest thrill of the Fair was a demonstration by inventor Elisha Otis. Otis was lifted high into the air on an open lift. At the highest point, the lift stopped. The crowd gasped as a man with an axe strode forward and chopped through the rope holding the lift. Instead of crashing to the ground, the lift stopped after just a few centimetres. It was stopped by the safety system that Otis had invented.

Several inventions came together in the late 1800s to produce the first skyscrapers. One of them was Otis's safety elevator (lift). New materials and new building techniques also helped to make skyscrapers possible.

At the Harbour Center in Vancouver, Canada, two lifts on the outside of the building offer a quick ride to the top.

A steel and concrete frame

Steel and concrete were not really new materials in the 1800s. Both had been used even before Roman times. However, in the 1800s it became possible to produce large amounts of steel cheaply. And reinforcing concrete with steel bars made it a much more useful building material.

In most buildings, the walls at the base have to be strong enough to support all the floors above. The taller a building gets, the thicker the walls must be. Above a certain height, the walls get so thick that they take up a lot of the space inside the building.

The first skyscrapers solved this problem by spreading the weight right across the building. The buildings had a framework of upright pillars and horizontal beams. The outer walls became a thin "skin" because they no longer had to support any weight.

Skyscrapers cluster together in Hong Kong, where land is in short supply.

The John Hancock Center in Chicago, USA has an outer frame that is strengthened by huge X-shaped braces. The building was an early tubular design by the engineer Fazlur Khan.

Giant tubes

The framework structure for skyscrapers worked very well for over 60 years. However, there was a limit on how high they could go. The problem was that the frame structure was not stiff enough. Really tall frame skyscrapers would sway alarmingly in strong winds.

In 1965, an engineer called Fazlur Khan came up with a solution to the problem. He built a 43-storey skyscraper with most of the support framework on the outside. It was like a hollow tube, so it was known as a tubular structure. The tubular design made the building much stiffer than a framed building.

In 1974, Khan designed the Sears Tower in Chicago. For a time, this was the tallest skyscraper in the world. Most other super-tall skyscrapers have been built using variations on the tubular structure.

Lighting and cooling

It takes a lot of energy (electricity, gas, or other fuel) to make skyscrapers comfortable places to work in. In most large skyscrapers, many rooms do not get any natural light. This means that the lights have to be on even during the daytime. Also, the thousands of people and machines in a skyscraper **generate** (produce) a lot of heat. Powerful air conditioning systems are needed to keep the temperature down.

ENVIRONMENTAL IMPACT: A BETTER PLACE TO WORK

The Commerzbank tower in Frankfurt, Germany has solved some of the lighting and cooling problems of most skyscrapers. The triangular skyscraper has a central "well" which lets air and light into the middle of the building. At nine levels there are large "sky gardens". This means that in most parts of the building, people can look out on a garden area. A special heating and cooling system also cuts down on energy bills.

This skyscraper in Canary Wharf in London uses plants inside the building to make it more pleasant.

BURJ KHALIFA

In 2010, the Burj Khalifa (Khalifa Tower) in Dubai in the Middle East was completed. It is the tallest skyscraper in the world. The tower is 828 metres (2,717 feet) tall. This is over 300 metres (nearly 1,000 feet) taller than any other skyscraper.

From the bottom up

Getting the foundations right is important for any skyscraper. The Burj Khalifa is built upon a massive "raft" of concrete, 3.7 metres (12 feet) thick. Huge concrete **piles** (posts), each 43 metres (141 feet) long, anchor the concrete raft deep in the ground. Over 100,000 tonnes of concrete were poured for the foundations of the Burj Khalifa.

Burj Khalifa has space for 1,044 luxury apartments, 49 floors of offices, and a 160-room hotel.

Y-shaped building

The ground plan of the Burj Khalifa is Y-shaped. This is a very good shape for a skyscraper, because it gives more window area. The shape is also good for supporting its huge height. The "arms" of the Y shape act as **buttresses**, or supports, for the central part of the building.

ENVIRONMENTAL IMPACT: GREEDY FOR ENERGY

The Burj Khalifa needs huge amounts of energy to keep it ticking over. On an average day it uses nearly one million litres (264,000 gallons) of water. When full, the building will use the same amount of electricity as about 10,500 homes.

It takes a team of 36 window cleaners 3 to 4 months to clean the Burj Khalifa's 24,348 windows. The top 27 floors are cleaned by an automatic machine.

BRIGHT IDEAS: SUPER LIFTS

The Burj Khalifa has record-breaking lifts. They are "double-decker" lifts, with two cabs one above the other. People can get into the lift on two floors at the same time. The lifts are the fastest ever. Speeding at 10 metres (33 feet) per second, the lifts take less than a minute to go from ground level to the 124th floor.

BUILDING NEW HOMES

On a building site in Northampton, lorries arrive, carrying large frameworks of wood or steel. A group of these frames joined together make the skeleton of a house. The kitchen and bathroom arrive as complete rooms, painted and ready to use. The outside is finished with lightweight panels. This is modern house-building.

Using less energy

Most houses waste large amounts of energy. They "leak" energy through thin glass windows and poorly fitting doors, up chimneys, and through the roof. A lot of the energy we use comes from burning **fossil fuels** such as oil and natural gas. Burning fossil fuels produces air pollution and is a major cause of **climate change**. Cutting down the amount of energy we waste in buildings would help to reduce climate change.

Greenwich Millennium Village is a modern housing estate being built in south-east London.

House factories

Traditionally, houses are built on-site, using bricks, stone, or similar materials. But for some new houses, large sections are built in factories. These factory-produced sections can range from individual wall panels to complete houses.

Building large sections of a house in a factory has many advantages. Parts can be cut by computer-controlled machines and fitted together with great accuracy. Doors and windows fit snugly and do not let in the wind. The whole building needs less looking after. At the building site there is less work to do, so houses can be built more quickly and easily.

Sometimes tents are the only homes that people can have if they need them quickly. These tents were put up after the 2010 earthquake in Haiti.

BRIGHT IDEAS: LOW-ENERGY MATERIALS

Some building materials take a lot of energy to produce. Aluminium, for example, needs huge amounts of electricity to process it into a building material. Architects designing low-energy buildings try to keep the energy costs of the materials low. They try to use materials that take little energy to produce, like wood. They may also use recycled materials, such as bricks from an old building.

Low-energy houses

Energy use can be cut down if houses are well-designed and built. Extra **insulation** (material used to prevent heat loss) and windows with two or three layers of glass can reduce the energy lost to the surroundings. Using factory-built house sections can help, too (see page 25).

The design of a building can make a huge difference to its energy use. Houses can be designed so that in summer hot air rises naturally out of the building, and cooler air is drawn in to take its place. In winter, devices called **heat exchangers** take heat from warm air escaping from the house, and use it to warm up the air coming in from outside.

Low-energy houses can also produce some of their own energy. They can have solar cells on the roof. These would make electricity from sunlight. Solar panels would use the Sun's power to heat water. Low-energy houses generally cost more to design and build than ordinary houses. However, savings on fuel bills can quickly make up for the extra building costs.

The solar panels on this low-energy house generate more than enough electricity to run the lights and other appliances.

The California Academy of Sciences in the United States has a "green roof", where plants grow in a layer of soil. The roof helps to keep the building cool in summer and warm in winter.

BRIGHT IDEAS: LEARNING FROM TERMITES

Millions of termites live together in huge termite mounds. To keep the mounds cool, the termites use natural "air conditioning". Warm air is drawn up and out of the mound through tall chimneys. Architects and engineers have used this idea to help cool down large buildings.

BRIGHT IDEAS: A "GREEN" SKYSCRAPER

The Bahrain World Trade Center is one of the world's first low-energy skyscrapers. Bahrain is very hot, so the building has to be kept cool. Special glass and window shades cut down the heat getting in through the windows. The building is cooled by a system that uses seawater. The skyscraper also produces some of its own electricity using three large wind turbines (windmills).

27

EARTHQUAKE PROOFING

On 17 January 1995, a powerful earthquake hit the areas around the city of Kobe, Japan. The earthquake lasted for only 20 seconds, but it killed over 6,400 people.

Building in earthquake zones

All around the world there are cities and towns built in earthquake zones. The buildings, bridges, and other structures need to be able to survive earthquakes. These buildings have to be strong. They are built with deep foundations and thick walls. Steel rods are often used to "tie together" building supports.

For large buildings and structures, simple strengthening is not enough. Often they are protected using a system called "base isolation". The foundations of the building (the base) are not fastened directly into the ground. Instead they "float" on springs or rubber pads, which cushion the building from the shaking of the Earth.

Buildings have to have a "buffer zone" around them to avoid them hitting other buildings during an earthquake.

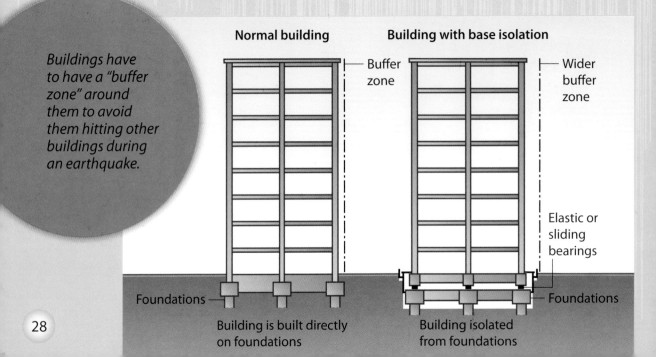

Normal building

Building with base isolation

Buffer zone

Wider buffer zone

Elastic or sliding bearings

Foundations

Foundations

Building is built directly on foundations

Building isolated from foundations

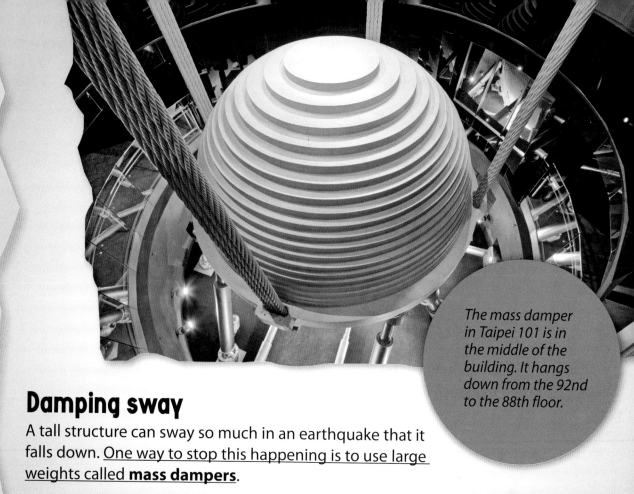

The mass damper in Taipei 101 is in the middle of the building. It hangs down from the 92nd to the 88th floor.

Damping sway

A tall structure can sway so much in an earthquake that it falls down. <u>One way to stop this happening is to use large weights called **mass dampers**</u>.

The mass damper in the skyscraper Taipei 101 is a huge steel ball weighing 660 tonnes. If the skyscraper starts to sway, the mass damper starts to swing. But as the building goes one way, the mass damper swings in the opposite direction. The swing of the pendulum partly cancels out the sway of the building. The result is that the building's sway is damped (reduced).

BRIGHT IDEAS: BUILT TO LAST

The Incas of Peru built stone buildings without using cement. The blocks of stone fitted together so well that not even a grass blade would go between them. Some of these Inca buildings have withstood earthquakes for hundreds of years.

HOLDING BACK THE RIVER

Dams are perhaps the biggest of all engineering projects. They can take ten years or more to build. A dam controls the flow of a river. It can control floods, provide drinking water, and allow bigger boats to travel upstream. Water from a dam can be used to generate electricity, or to **irrigate** (water) farm crops.

Dams also have unwanted effects. When a dam is built, a large area of land is flooded. Thousands of people may lose their homes, and the **reservoir** (lake behind the dam) destroys the habitat of many plants and animals.

Penstocks and spillways

Dams have several kinds of channels (passageways) and openings to let water through.

- A spillway is a channel where water can escape once it reaches a certain height. Spillways act like the overflow on a sink.
- For hydroelectric power, water is channelled along pipes called penstocks. They feed water to turbines that turn electric generators.
- For irrigation, water from the reservoir is fed into a system of canals (see pages 34 to 37).

The Tarbela Dam in Pakistan is one of the biggest embankment dams in the world.

Types of dam

The most common kind of dam is an **embankment dam**. This is a large pile of compressed (squashed down) earth or rocks built across the river. An embankment dam has to include a waterproof layer to stop the water from simply soaking through it.

Other types of dam are built from concrete or masonry (brick or stone). A concrete **gravity dam** holds back the water through sheer weight. The dam is very thick at the base and much thinner at the top.

A **buttress dam** has a thinner wall than a simple gravity dam. Triangular supports called buttresses prop up the downstream side of the dam.

Arch dams have the thinnest wall of any dam type. The dam is shaped like an arch pointing upstream. The arched shape transfers the main weight of the water outwards to the rocky sides of the valley.

Kaprun Dam in the Austrian Alps is a concrete arch dam. Arch dams can only be built across narrow valleys with solid, rocky sides.

The Itaipú Dam

The Itaipú Dam is on the Paraná River, on the border between Brazil and Paraguay. It is the biggest hollow gravity dam in the world. The dam itself is 196 metres (643 feet) tall, and nearly 8 kilometres (5 miles) long. This is 18 times bigger than the Hoover Dam in the United States. It holds back the water by sheer weight – about 60 million tonnes. The 20 electricity generators powered by the dam produce more electricity each year than any other dam.

Glen Canyon Dam in Arizona, USA is a concrete arch dam on the Colorado River.

BRIGHT IDEAS: LOCKS AND LADDERS

A dam is an obstacle to anything travelling up or down the river. Dams on large rivers often have a set of locks (see pages 36 and 37) that allow boats to travel around the dam. A dam may also have a fish ladder. This is a channel that drops down from the top of the dam in a series of small steps. Most fish can swim down the steps, and species such as salmon can get upstream by jumping up the steps.

These satellite photos show the areas that were flooded after the Three Gorges Dam in China was built.

Three Gorges Dam

ENVIRONMENTAL IMPACT: MAKING SACRIFICES

The Itaipú Dam took 40,000 workers seven years to build. Three years of this time were taken up with diverting (moving) part of the river along a specially dug channel. About 10,000 people were forced to move from their homes for the Itaipu project. The Guaíra Falls, one of the largest waterfalls in the world, was drowned by the reservoir behind the dam.

CANALS

The oil tanker is 304 metres (997 feet) long and 32 metres (105 feet) wide. It will only just fit into the canal lock. Fully loaded, the tanker weighs 60,000 tonnes. Any mistake would be a disaster.

The crew throw cables to the shore on either side. The cables are fastened to small, powerful train engines. As the tanker inches forwards, the train engines pull on the cables. They help to keep the tanker in the centre of the channel. After several tense minutes, the tanker stops. It is now ready to make its trip through the Panama Canal.

What is a canal?

A canal is an artificial waterway. In the past, many canals were built because boats were the only way to move really heavy loads from place to place. Today, trains and lorries can haul heavy loads, too. But some large canals are still important. The Panama Canal is one of these.

The biggest ships that can fit through the locks of the Panama Canal are about 305 metres (1,000 feet) long. Ships of this size are called "Panamax" ships.

Building the Panama Canal

The Panama Canal cuts through a thin neck of land dividing the Atlantic Ocean from the Pacific Ocean. Ships take 10 hours to sail through the canal. If it wasn't there, they would have a four-week trip around South America.

The Panama Canal was started by a team of French engineers in the 1880s. The French team did a lot of work, but nearly 22,000 workers died from fever. In the end they gave up the project. In 1905 the US government took over the canal. They spent the first two years improving working conditions and far fewer workers died from fever.

The Americans built a dam across the Chagres River to create a huge lake called Gatun Lake. The lake provided water to keep the canal full. At each end of the canal they built a set of three locks (see pages 36 and 37) to lift ships up to the level of Gatun Lake, then back down again.

Heavy machinery is used to expand the Panama Canal in 2009, ten years after the USA handed over control of the canal to the country of Panama.

How canals work

Some canals are simply stretches of river that have been straightened or dredged (dug out) so that larger boats can use them. Other canals are built to connect two rivers across a range of hills – or to connect two oceans, like the Panama Canal. These are called **summit canals**. A canal has to be level, or all the water will quickly run out of it. But a summit canal needs to climb over hills. How can it do this?

WHO DID THAT? CANAL GATES

The gates across a lock are called **mitre gates**. They meet at an angle, like an arrow pointing upstream. This design helps the gates stay shut when water presses on them. The Italian artist Leonardo da Vinci (1452–1519) is thought to have invented mitre gates, for the San Marco Lock in Milan.

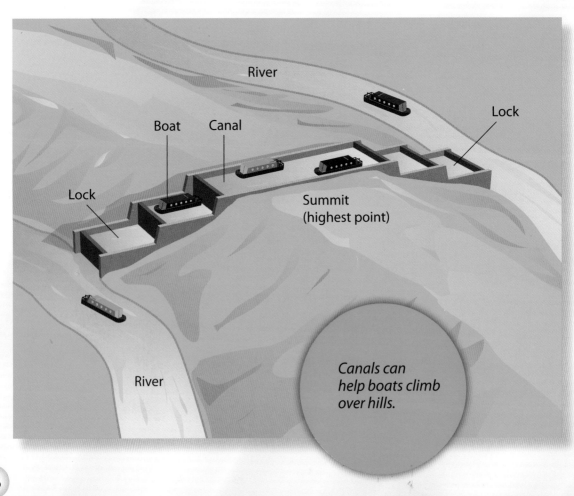

River

Boat

Canal

Lock

Lock

Summit (highest point)

River

Canals can help boats climb over hills.

Climbing in steps

To change level, a canal uses locks. Locks are like steps. The stretch of canal between two locks is level. But as it goes through a lock, the canal goes up or down one step. A lock is a short water channel with heavy gates at either end. The stretch of water on one side of the lock is higher than the stretch on the other side.

A boat going up the canal enters the lock at the lower level. The lower gates shut, then water from the higher level is allowed in. The lock fills to the higher level and the boat floats up with it. The higher lock gates are then opened and the boat can sail on.

A canal with locks needs a source of water at the highest level, to keep it full. This is because every time a lock is used, water flows from the higher level to the lower level. To keep the canal working, the higher level has to be filled up.

The Falkirk Wheel in Scotland is a rotating boat lift. The lift uses far less water than a canal.

GOING UNDER GROUND

In Boston Harbor in the United States, the biggest floating digger in the world is at work. It is digging an underwater trench which will hold a tunnel. The tunnel itself is being built in sections, 650 kilometres away. Each section is 100 metres (328 feet) long and weighs 33,000 tonnes. The sections are floated up the coast to Boston and sunk into the trench. But there is a problem. Despite careful planning, the tunnel is one metre too short! An extra piece has to be added in a hurry. Even engineers get it wrong sometimes.

The tunnel under Boston Harbor was part of a project called the Big Dig. This moved large amounts of Boston's traffic into underground tunnels.

Building tunnels

Tunnels can carry traffic beneath a crowded city, dive under a river, or punch a route through a mountain. The first step in building a tunnel is to look at the rocks. A tunnel running through hard rock such as **granite** needs less support than soft rock. But hard rock is really tough to cut. Softer sandy rocks or **shale** are much easier to tunnel through. However, without support, the tunnel will collapse.

Tunnel boring machines

Modern tunnels are often built using machines called TBMs (tunnel boring machines). Each TBM has a massive rotating cutting head at the front. As the TBM digs the tunnel, it puts in a strong lining to support the weight of rock above the tunnel. Shallow tunnels can be built another way, called "cut and cover". Engineers dig a deep trench, and build the tunnel at the bottom. They then cover the tunnel over with earth and rock.

The front end of this giant boring machine has a rotating cutting head. It is 10 metres (33 feet) across.

THE STRUCTURES OF THE FUTURE

What will the structures of the future be like? Some projects are already in the pipeline, and we can see how they may turn out. Looking further ahead, engineers will probably be using amazing materials and building whole cities designed to save energy.

Plans in the pipeline

One of the biggest engineering projects now being carried out is a tunnel underneath the Swiss Alps. When it is completed in 2017, the Gotthard Base Tunnel will be 57 kilometres (35 miles) long. It will be the longest rail tunnel in the world.

This is the design for an eco-city that is ecologically friendly and self-sufficient in water and energy.

In China, several massive dams are transforming the Yangtze River. The Three Gorges Dam on the lower Yangtze River is complete. This huge dam can produce 22,500 megawatts of power. Several other dams almost as big are being built on the upper part of the Yangtze.

Several skyscrapers taller than the Burj Khalifa are being planned. In Kuwait in the Middle East, there are plans for a twisting triple tower 1,001 metres (3,284 feet) tall. An even taller skyscraper called the Nakheel Tower is planned for Dubai, also in the Middle East.

Low-energy building is almost certain to be important in the future. In a desert area in Abu Dhabi in the Middle East, a city called Masdar is being built. Masdar will be powered mainly by solar energy. Narrow streets will prevent buildings getting too much sunlight, and special materials will let in cool breezes but not heat. Below ground, small electric cars will speed people from place to place.

Plans for the future

Further in the future, it is more difficult to know what actual structures will be built. However, there are some clear trends. New materials are changing engineering. **Composites** are materials made by mixing very strong fibres together with tough plastic. They are much lighter than concrete or steel, but just as strong. In the future, record-breaking bridges and other structures could be built with composite materials.

FACT FILE

RECORD-BREAKING BRIDGES

World's longest bridge: Weihe Grand Bridge in China, nearly 80 kilometres (50 miles) long. It carries a high-speed rail link between the cities of Zhengzhou and Xi'an.

Longest sea bridge: Hangzhou Bay Bridge, linking Shanghai with the city of Ningbo, China. It is 35.6 kilometres (22 miles) long.

Longest single-span bridge: Akashi Kaikyo Bridge, linking the Honshu and Awaji Islands, Japan has a central span 1,991 metres (6,532 feet) long.

Longest arch bridge: Chaotianmen Bridge over Yangtze River, China. Its central arch span is 552 metres (1,811 feet) long.

World's tallest bridge: Millau Viaduct, over River Tarn Gorge, France. The tallest pillar is 343 metres (1,125 ft) tall.

TOP TEN TALLEST SKYSCRAPERS

Burj Khalifa, Dubai, Middle East (completed 2010): 828 metres (2717 feet).

Taipei 101, Taipei, Taiwan (completed 2004): 509 metres (1670 feet).

Shanghai World Financial Center, Shanghai, China (completed 2008): 492 metres (1614 feet).

International Commerce Centre, Kowloon, Hong Kong, China (completed 2010): 484 metres (1588 feet).

Petronas Towers, Kuala Lumpur, Malaysia (completed 1998): 452 metres (1483 feet).

Nanjing Greenland Financial Center, Nanjing, China (completed 2010): 450 metres (1476 feet).

Willis Tower, Chicago, USA (completed 1974): 442 metres (1450 feet).

Guangzhou International Finance Centre, Guangzhou, China (completed 2010): 440 metres (1444 feet).

Jin Mao Building, Shanghai, China (completed 1999): 421 metres (1381 feet).

Two International Finance Centre, Hong Kong (completed 2003): 415 metres (1362 feet).

RECORD-BREAKING DAMS

Dam containing most material: Syncrude Tailings Dam, Canada.
The dam contains 540 million cubic metres (706 million cubic yards)
of material.

Tallest dam: Nurek Dam in Tajikistan, 300 metres (984 feet) tall.

Longest dam: Hirakud Dam, India, 26 kilometres (16 miles) in length.

Biggest reservoir: The Itaipú Dam holds back more water than any
other dam in the world. Lake Volta in Uganda is the reservoir that
covers the biggest area.

Most electricity: The Itaipú Dam produced the most electricity in
one year. The Three Gorges Dam, China produces the most power
from its generators.

CANAL RECORD-BREAKERS

World's longest canal: Grand Canal in China, 1,775 kilometres
(1,115 miles) long.

Largest canal lock: Berendrecht Lock in Antwerp, Belgium, 500 metres
(1,640 feet) long and 68 metres (223 feet) wide.

Longest canal tunnel: Le Grand Souterrain on the St Quentin Canal,
France, 5.7 kilometres (3½ miles) long.

Deepest canal: Corinth Canal, Greece. It cuts through the Isthmus
of Corinth at a depth of 52 metres (171 feet).

TUNNELS

Longest tunnel of any kind: Delaware Tunnel in New York, USA, 137
kilometres (85 miles) long. It carries water.

Longest road or rail tunnel: Seikan railway tunnel in Japan, 53.9 kilometres
(33.5 miles) long; 23.3 kilometre (14½ miles) of the tunnel is under water.

Longest underwater road or rail tunnel: Channel Tunnel, linking UK and
France, 50.5 kilometres (31.4 miles) long; 37.9 kilometres (23.5 miles)
of the tunnel is underwater.

Longest road tunnel: Lærdal Tunnel, Norway, 24.5 kilometres
(15.2 miles) long.

Glossary

arch dam dam with fairly thin concrete walls, with an arched shape that helps hold back the water behind the dam

buttress angled supports used to hold up a wall, a dam or other structure

buttress dam concrete dam that has a thinner wall than a gravity dam, which is supported by buttresses

climate change gradual change in the general weather around the world, which is getting warmer due to pollution caused by human activities

composite material made up of fibres of very strong but brittle material embedded in a tough plastic resin

deck part of a bridge that carries the road or railway track

embankment dam dam made from piled up earth or rocks

engineer person who uses maths and scientific knowledge to solve practical problems

fibreglass material in which thin glass fibres are embedded in a tough plastic resin

fossil fuel fuel made from the remains of animals and/or plants that lived millions of years ago. Oil, gas, and coal are all fossil fuels.

foundation underlying base of a building or bridge

generate produce

geodesic dome dome made up of interlocking triangular sections

gorge deep, steep-sided valley

granite type of hard rock formed from the cooling of molten rocks underground

gravity dam dam that holds back the water behind it through sheer weight

hangers cables used to hang the deck of a suspension bridge

heat exchanger device that takes heat from warm air leaving a building and uses it to warm up cooler air coming into the building

Incas tribe of people from Peru in South America that in the 15th century built a large empire centred on the Andes mountains

insulation in buildings, materials that are used to prevent heat escaping from the building

irrigate to water farm crops

lock short section of a canal with watertight gates at either end, which allows the canal to change level

mass damper heavy weight put into a tall building or other structure that helps to stop the structure shaking itself apart in an earthquake

mitre gate type of gate used in most canal locks, which form a V-shape pointing upstream when closed

pile column or pillar sunk into the ground

reinforced concrete concrete with steel bars embedded in it to make it stronger

reservoir lake behind a dam

shale type of soft rock formed from layers of clay

summit canal canal that connects two rivers across a range of hills, or connects two sections of sea separated by land

suspension bridge bridge that can span large gaps with no ground support

turbine engine that has blades that are made to spin by water, wind, or steam

Find out more

Books

Airports (Buildings at Work), Elizabeth Encarnacion (QED, 2007)

Building Amazing Structures series, Chris Oxlade (Heinemann Library, 2007)

Sports Stadiums (Buildings at Work), Elizabeth Encarnacion (QED, 2007)

Skyscrapers (Buildings at Work), Elizabeth Encarnacion (QED, 2007)

The Story Behind Skyscrapers (True Stories), Sean Stewart Price (Heinemann Library, 2009).

Websites

Building big
www.pbs.org/wgbh/buildingbig
This website is based on a series of US TV programmes about bridges, domes, skyscrapers, dams, and tunnels.

Structures
www.technologystudent.com/struct1/struindex.htm
This website has lots of information on bridges and towers, including ideas for building bridges out of modelling straws.

Panama Canal History Museum
www.canalmuseum.com
This contains photos, documents, books, and stories of the Panama Canal.

Bridge basics: a spotter's guide to bridge design
www.pghbridges.com/basics.htm
This gives you information about a huge range of different kinds of bridge. What types can you spot in your area?

Wonderful houses around the world
www.shelterpub.com/_wonderful_houses/wh-toc.html
This shows a range of interesting houses from different parts of
the world.

The low-energy house
 www.lowenergyhouse.com
This is an introduction to building low-energy houses
and buildings.

Tacoma Narrows
www.youtube.com/watch?v=P0Fi1VcbpAI
Watch the film of the first Tacoma Narrows Bridge shaking itself
to bits in 1940.

Centuries of civil engineering
www.lindahall.org/events_exhib/exhibit/exhibits/civil/index.shtml
Find out about the history of bridges, monuments, lighthouses,
viaducts, and other mega-structures of the past.

Topics for research

Building airports
Find out about Hong Kong airport, and Kansai Airport in Osaka, Japan.

Oil refineries
Investigate oil refineries to see how big they are. How much area do
they cover? How does that compare to a sports field, for example?

Taisun, the world's biggest crane
Find out how this crane is used by the oil industry.

Index